for my children

When I go to Mass

By Sarah Hlavacek

This is our Church.

It is the house of God.

We come here to be with Jesus,

to pray, to worship and to offer

the Great Sacrifice of the Mass.

Today we are here for Sunday Mass.
Let's go inside.

When I go to mass I need to make myself ready...

I Make the Sign of the Cross

I bless myself with Holy Water,

"In the name of the Father and of the Son and of

the Holy Spirit. Amen." God is with me.

When I go to mass...

I Genuflect

I show Jesus with my body

that I love him. By making my body small,

I say you are so great my Lord.

When I go to mass...

I Prepare My Heart

I kneel down and make my body still.

I speak to God and

open my heart to Him.

When I go to mass...

I Sing

I show Jesus with my voice that
I love Him. I sing hymns and I sing prayers.
I sing with joy to Jesus.

When I go to mass...

I Listen To God's Word

I hear the readings from the Holy Bible.
I listen.
God speaks to my heart.

When I go to mass...

I See Bread and Wine

I see the cruets of wine and water.

I see the hosts of bread.

These are our gifts.

I see them being brought to the altar.

When I go to mass...

I See the Chalice and the Paten

I see the Chalice, that holds the wine
that becomes Jesus. I see the Paten, that holds the
bread that becomes Jesus. These will be part of our
Great Sacrifice.

When I go to mass...

The Holy Spirit Comes

The priest prays to God and stretches
out his hands like this. The Holy Spirit comes.
He blesses the gifts and makes them Holy.

When I go to mass...

The Bread Becomes Jesus

The priest says the words Jesus

spoke at the Last Supper.

"This is My body. Given up for you.."

The bread

becomes Jesus.

He is offered

up for me.

When I go to mass...

The Wine Becomes Jesus

The priest says the words Jesus

spoke at the Last Supper.

"This is My blood poured out for you.."

The wine

becomes Jesus.

His mercy is poured

out on me.

When I go to mass...

I See Jesus in the Eucharist

The bread and wine have become Jesus.

We now call them "The Eucharist"

When I go to mass...

Jesus Finds A Home in My Heart

When I eat the Eucharist,

Jesus comes to live within me.

My heart becomes His home.

When I go to mass...

I Say Thank you

I say thank you to Jesus for coming to me in the Eucharist. I thank Him for all He has done for me and all He has given me.

When mass has ended...

I Am Sent Forth

The priest blesses me "In the name
of the Father and the Son and the Holy Spirit.
Amen." God is with me.

When I leave mass...

I Share God's Love With All Those I Meet...